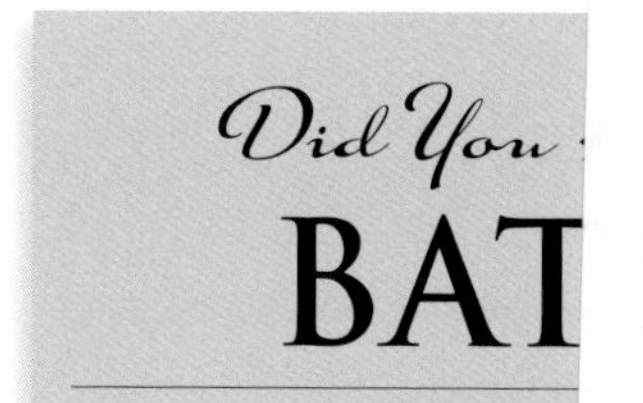

Compiled by Julia Skinner

With particular reference to the work of Martin Andrew

THE FRANCIS FRITH COLLECTION

www.francisfrith.com

First published in the United Kingdom in 2006 by The Francis Frith Collection®

This edition published exclusively for Oakridge in 2010 ISBN 978-1-84589-522-8

British Library Cataloguing in Publication Data

Did You Know? Bath - A Miscellany
Compiled by Julia Skinner
With particular reference to the work of Martin Andrew

The Francis Frith Collection
Frith's Barn, Teffont,
Salisbury, Wiltshire SP3 5QP
Tel: +44 (0) 1722 716 376
Email: info@francisfrith.co.uk
www.francisfrith.com

Printed and bound in Malaysia

Front Cover: **BATH, UNION STREET 1923** 73964p

The colour-tinting is for illustrative purposes only, and is not intended to be historically accurate

AS WITH ANY HISTORICAL DATABASE, THE FRANCIS FRITH ARCHIVE IS CONSTANTLY BEING CORRECTED AND IMPROVED, AND THE PUBLISHERS WOULD WELCOME INFORMATION ON OMISSIONS OR INACCURACIES

CONTENTS

INTRODUCTION

'Oh, who can ever be tired of Bath?'
(Jane Austen, 'Northanger Abbey')

The elegant city of Bath ranks as one of the most popular destinations for visitors to Britain. Modern tourism can perhaps be traced back to the beginning of the 18th century with the appointment of the dandy Richard 'Beau' Nash as Master of Ceremonies to the spa resort of Bath. Although Bath had attracted a steady stream of visitors over the centuries, seeking relief from the curative property of its waters, the city had become so dirty and infested that the afflicted were in danger of exchanging one disease for another. Nash set to work cleaning up the place, and success followed almost immediately, with Bath attracting not only the leading socialites of the day, but also men of ideas and resources. Their investment created a city that is now regarded as one of the finest architectural achievements of its age, and which has sometimes been dubbed 'Florence on Avon'. John Wood the Elder and John Wood the Younger - father and son - were responsible for much of the new city's architecture, and it was the inspiration of John the Younger that conceived the magnificent crescents for which Bath is famous. The city is now designated a UNESCO World Heritage Site.

Ironically, Bath's prominence as a fashionable spa town during the 18th century was achieved without any inkling of what lay beneath the pavements - the ancient Roman baths. Although the area of hot springs was probably already sacred to the Celtic people of pre-Roman Britain, it was the Romans who first exploited the site by building their town of Aquae Sulis here. At the end of the Roman period the baths became covered with mud, and were not rediscovered until the late 19th century.

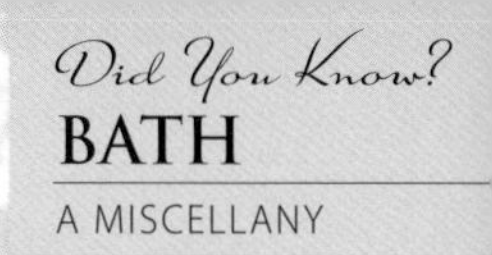

Bath is now a bustling modern city, lively with students and thronged with tourists, and is an exciting place in which to live and work. Its story is full of fascinating characters and events, of which this book can only provide a brief glimpse.

THE ABBEY 1911 63682

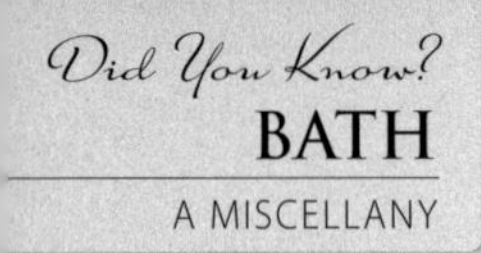

NORTH SOMERSET DIALECT WORDS AND PHRASES CONNECTED WITH BATH

'Dimpsey' - twilight, dusk.

'Dumbledore' - bumblebee.

'Addled' - gone off, rancid.

'Bide' - stay.

'Ow bist?'- how are you?

'Cradlehood' - infancy.

'Crousty'- bad tempered.

'Nottled'or 'nottling' - really cold.

'Banes' - jocular expression for the area of Bath and North-East Somerset, ie 'I live in Banes'.

In Chaucer's 'The Canterbury Tales', the Wife of Bath uses the phrase 'as drunk as a mouse' to insult her husband: 'Thou comest hoom as dronken as a mous'. This derives from the habit mice had in medieval times of falling into beer vats.

In Bath's heyday as a centre for 'taking the waters', society people would engage 'aquatic doctors' to prescribe the proper dose of the mineral water for their afflictions. This is the origin of the slang word 'quack' for a doctor.

In the 18th and 19th centuries, the expression 'Off with you to Bath!' was a way of saying that someone was acting stupidly, or an accusation of insanity, as so many people suffering from physical or mental ailments came to the city in hopes of a cure.

HAUNTED BATH

Next to the Theatre Royal stands the Garrick Head Pub, which is reputed to be haunted by at least two ghosts. The ghost of a regency rake hovers near the entrance. A strong scent of perfume has been reported in the cellar, and it has been suggested that this may have a link with the ghost of a lady who committed suicide when her gambling lover lost a duel in which she was the prize. The building also has a Grey Lady, believed to be the spectre of a lady who died when she threw herself out of a window; her ghost is also said to sometimes be seen sitting in a box in the Theatre Royal.

Plague victims are said to have been buried at the bottom of a long drop below the road opposite the Theatre Royal; the medieval wall there marked the edge of the old city. Legend says that the sounds of wailing and groaning can sometimes be heard in the area.

The ghost of a woman in an old-fashioned dress and bonnet has been reported in a building in Grosvenor Place.

The George in Bathampton is reputed be haunted by the ghost of Jean Baptiste Du Barre, an 18th-century Frenchman who was carried there to die after fighting a duel. He has allegedly been seen leaning on the bar on the anniversary of his death!

The Beehive pub in Lansdowne Road has a ghostly barmaid affectionately known as Bunty, who opens and shuts doors and rattles saucepans.

One of Bath's best-known ghosts is that of a man in 18th-century clothes and a black hat, who is believed to roam around near the Assembly Rooms, Saville Row and Bennett Street.

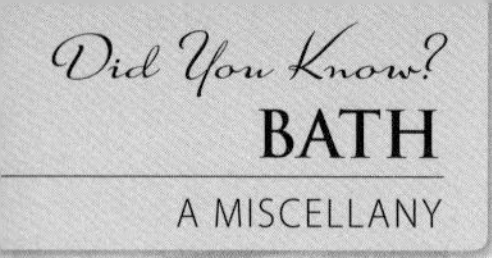

BATH MISCELLANY

The hot springs at Bath issue forth over a quarter of a million gallons of water every day, and must have appeared a marvel in ancient times. It seems that at the time of the Roman conquest of Britain, the springs of Bath were sacred to the Celtic goddess Sul. Her name was retained in the name of the Roman town, Aquae Sulis ('The Waters of Sul'), although the goddess herself was assimilated into the Roman goddess Minerva.

During the Roman period, the fame of 'the waters of Sul' spread throughout Britannia and northern Gaul (modern day France). Thousands of people flocked here for cures, for rheumatic diseases in particular. The Romans built a very impressive collection of bath houses and pool buildings, over 350ft long by 150ft wide. There was an oval, a circular and a square bath, but the largest, a rectangular one, was only rediscovered in 1880. Lead-lined, it had steps into it from the sides and was surrounded by colonnades. Later it was vaulted over with stone. The bases of the piers remain, and also the bath itself, which is fed by hot springs by a constant 50 degrees Celsius. In 1897 John Brydon constructed an appropriately Roman-style building around the newly discovered bath, open to the sky.

Milsom Street is now one of Bath's most famous shopping streets, but when it was originally built in the 1760s it was intended to be a row of elegant houses, designed by the architect John Wood the Younger. It was one of the earlier streets laid out beyond the boundaries of the original walled town. It only acquired shops from about 1800 onwards.

THE ABBEY, THE WEST FRONT 1887 19583

THE ROMAN BATHS,
THE SCULPTURE FROM THE TEMPLE OF SUL-MINERVA 1907 57725

There was an important temple at the Roman town of Aquae Sulis, dedicated to Sul-Minerva. Fragments of the temple have come to light, and by far the most important of these were the remnants of its main pediment, found in 1790 during building works for Thomas Baldwin's Pump Room (see photograph 57725, above). It is of the highest, indeed metropolitan, quality, and depicts the snake-haired and bearded Gorgon's head on the shield of Minerva, which is supported by two winged Victories.

The Roman road known as the Fosse Way ran right through Bath on its way from Lincoln to Axminster in Devon. It was built as a military road around AD47.

The Anglo-Saxon name for the town was Bathum, (or Bathan, or Bathon), which meant 'at the baths', from which the present name is derived. In AD675, Osric, the king of the Anglo-Saxon sub-kingdom of the Hwicce, set up a monastic house at Bath. This monastery came under the control of King Offa of Mercia in AD781, who rebuilt the church, which was dedicated to St Peter.

The area seen in photograph B33099 (below) was part of a reconstruction scheme in the 1790s. The statues of Romans and the balustrade to the right of the photograph were added in 1897, along with a colonnade around the Roman baths below.

YORK STREET AND THE ROMAN BATHS c1955 B33099

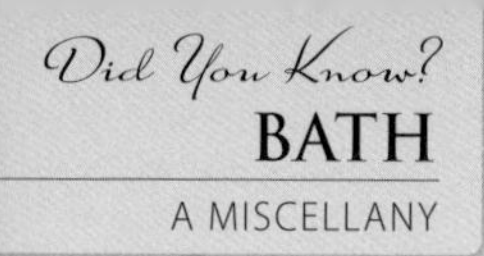

BATHEASTON, THE BRIDGE AND THE WEIR 1907 57750

The fine arched bridge at Batheaston seen in this photograph was built to serve a livestock market at neighbouring Bathampton. The toll-house still carries a board detailing the charges once levied: a score of pigs or sheep cost the same as a cart, 6d, while cattle and people were each charged ½d.

THE ROMAN BATHS 1890 25135

The fascinating view in photograph 25135 (above) shows the Roman baths before John Brydon's 1897 alterations and new buildings. Brydon added dignified colonnades around the baths, with balustrades and statues. The quality of Brydon's work is well brought out in photograph 46468 on page 38-39; visitors often comment on the remarkable survival of so much Roman work, not realising that this is mostly Victorian reconstruction. The Roman remains are the large stumps of piers that line the edges of the bath, which are linked by steps leading into the water.

The names of Northgate Street and Southgate Street commemorate the north and south gates of the medieval walled town of Bath.

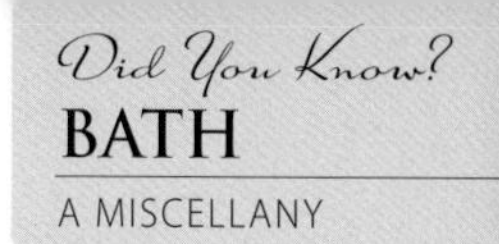

Bath's abbey was founded in the 9th century. It had a moment of glory when King Edgar was crowned here at a great assembly in May AD973. The event was noteworthy as Edgar was dubbed the first 'High King of all England'- before this, England was a heptarchy. The coronation ceremony was devised by Archbishop Dunstan and is still the basis of coronation ceremonies today; it consists of the recognition and oath, which is a form of contract sworn between the monarch and the people, and also the consecration of the monarch by anointment.

In 2004, a movie version of Thackeray's 'Vanity Fair', starring Reese Witherspoon as Becky Sharp, was largely filmed in Bath.

FROM RAINBOW WOODS 1929 82328

King William Rufus, son of William the Conqueror, granted the city of Bath to the royal physician John of Tours, who became Bishop of Wells and Abbot of Bath in 1088. He was granted permission to move the cathedra of the Bishop of the Somerset See from Wells to Bath, thus becoming the first Bishop of Bath, and a large Norman church was built. However, later bishops preferred to live at Wells, which regained cathedral status jointly with Bath, and by the 15th century, Bath's abbey church had become badly dilapidated.

In the last years of the 15th century, Oliver King, Bishop of Bath and Wells, had a dream in which he saw angels climbing up and down ladders to heaven whilst a voice called for a king to restore Bath's abbey church. Bishop King took the word 'king' to refer to himself, and commissioned the leading court architects of the day, Robert and William Vertue, to design a new abbey church; it rose slowly from 1499 onwards, a magnificent Perpendicular Gothic building with a fine central tower. The church was a victim of the Dissolution of the Monasteries in 1539, and work stuttered and stopped. The nave was only roofed (in timber rather than stone) in the early 17th century. The present stone vaults over the nave are 19th-century. The west front of the abbey church is famous for two ladders carved out of stone on each side of the west window, with angels ascending and descending, commemorating Bishop King's dream. They can be seen in photograph 19583 on page 7.

The present abbey church was built on the site of the Norman nave only; it is obviously much smaller than its great Norman predecessor, fragments of which remain incorporated in the east end.

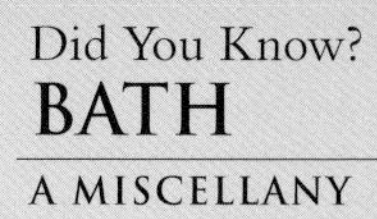

THE VIEW FROM THE ABBEY 1929 82323

MILSOM STREET 1925 76754

In the 18th century, Bath was in effect rebuilt, replanned and greatly expanded to accommodate the fashionable visitors who soon flocked there to take the waters, to gamble, to attend assemblies and generally to enjoy themselves for the Bath 'season'. Huge numbers of houses were built, mainly to rent to the visitors. Fortunes were made - and sometimes lost - by landowners, speculative builders and architects; one of the best architects to work in and for the city, Thomas Baldwin, went bankrupt. Baldwin designed one of the best buildings in Milsom Street, Somersetshire Buildings (1782), seen half-way down the street on the right of photograph 76754, above. This is a terrace of five houses, with pedimented end houses and a central house with a bowed front, all enriched with columns, capitals and cornices, and is a total contrast to the regular flat fronts of the other Georgian houses in the street.

Bath was described by one 18th-century writer as 'the busiest idle place in the world', where fashionable people of leisure flocked to indulge in drinking, dancing, billiards, gambling, gossiping, matchmaking, and a host of other demanding pursuits.

Several famous names from history have lived at the Circus in Bath: No 13 was the residence of the explorer and missionary David Livingstone (it is now a dental office). Lord Clive of India once lived next door, at No 14, and three doors down, at No 17, is where the artist Thomas Gainsborough is said to have painted his masterpiece, 'Blue Boy'.

THE CIRCUS 1911 63686

Just below Batheaston village a weir impedes the progress of the Avon, which served to impound water to power two mills. The mill shown in photograph 57751, below, is on the Bathampton (south)

bank of the Avon, and manufactured gunpowder; the other mill, on the northern bank, was used to grind corn. Both mills are still there today, but have been converted into restaurants.

BATHEASTON, THE WEIR 1907 57751

PULTENEY BRIDGE AND WEIR 1914 67451

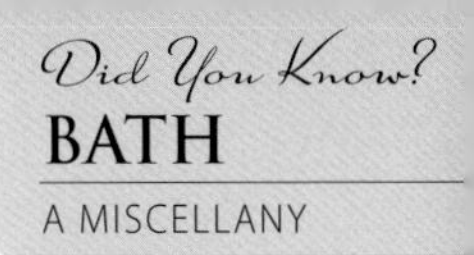

The Pump Room, completed in 1796, was where the sick and the socialites came to 'take the waters'. Dr William Oliver claimed that the Bath water would cure 'the itch, noise in the ears, running of the ears, sharpness of urine, wounds, ulcers, piles, numbness in any part and all special diseases of women.' Another doctor claimed it was a remedy for 'rheumatic, gouty and paralytic afflictions, in all those disorders originating from indigestion and acidity of the stomach, bilious and glandular obstructions, hypochondriac and hysterical afflictions', and Queen Anne took the waters in an attempt to alleviate dropsy. Visitors to Bath can try the hot spa water at the fountain in the Pump Room, but be warned - the water contains 43 minerals, but its sulphury flavour is not pleasant!

The oldest house in Bath can be found at 4 North Parade Passage; in the basement are remains of Roman, Saxon, and medieval architecture. The building currently houses Sally Lunn's tearooms and museum, traditionally supposed to be named after a French Huguenot refugee called Sally Lunn (her real name was probably Solange Luyon), who moved into the house in 1680 and became famous for baking her version of yeast-based teacakes. However, there are many other interpretations of the origin of the famous 'Sally Lunn cakes'; one says that Sally was the daughter of a pastry cook in Bath, and another that there was actually no one named Sally at all, and the name of the cakes comes from an old street cry in corrupted French, 'Solet lune', for 'sol et lune', the French words for sun and moon, which may have been used to describe the golden-topped buns.

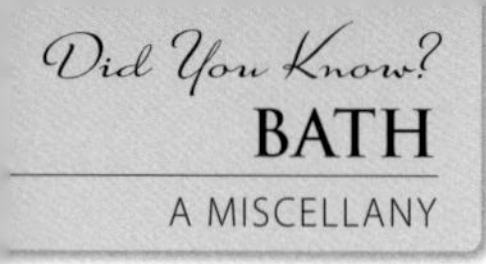

The building of Georgian Bath was largely due to the enterprise of a local postmaster, Ralph Allen, and the golden stone of Bath's famous buildings came from his quarries on Coombe Down. Ralph Allen (1693-1764) came to Bath in 1710 as a young man; he worked as a clerk in the Bath Post Office, and in 1712 he became the Post Master of Bath. He rose to have a successful career in the Post Office, and reformed the postal service by creating a network of postal roads that did not have to pass through London; it has been estimated that he saved the Post Office £1,500,000 over a 40 year period, and made a huge fortune for himself. He acquired the stone quarries at Coombe Down just as the building boom started in Bath, and by supplying the stone for the city's development he made himself a second fortune. He was a shrewd politician, active in local affairs, and became Mayor of Bath several times. He was also the Member of Parliament for Bath between 1757 and 1764. In 1742 he had a beautiful mansion (Prior Park) built for himself on a hill overlooking the city, 'To see all Bath, and for all Bath to see', but he also contributed to the city in other ways: he built cottages for the masons working in his quarries, he was a benefactor to the poor, and he donated both money and stone for the building of the Mineral Water Hospital in 1738. Ralph Allen died in 1764 at the age of 71, and is buried in a pyramid-topped tomb in Claverton churchyard. His name is commemorated in Bath by Ralph Allen Drive and Ralph Allen School.

ST MICHAEL'S CHURCH
1904 53000

QUEEN SQUARE c1955 B33117

John Wood the Elder began his attempt to turn the provincial city of Bath into 'New Rome' with Queen Square in 1728 (see photograph B33117, above), where he designed each side as what became known as 'palace fronts'. This was an idea he probably copied from terraces in London's Grosvenor Square. The terrace houses, usually three windows or bays wide, are built as if they are a vast palace façade with a centrepiece, usually pedimented, and with the end houses treated as end pavilions. This rapidly became the norm for similar developments, not only in Bath but also elsewhere in England, and helped significantly in giving the townscape great dignity and coherence. John Wood the Elder also built the 'Grand Place of Assembly to be called the Great Forum of Bath', now called (rather less grandiosely) North Parade and South Parade, and much else besides. His other great design was the King's Circus, now just called the Circus; he had just started building the Circus when he died in 1754, and the work was taken over and completed by his son, also called John (see photograph 63686, page 17).

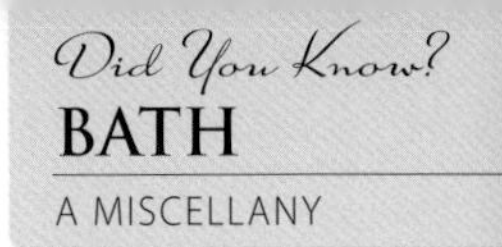

Charles Dickens featured Bath in 'The Pickwick Papers', and poked fun at the city's social life. In the book, Mr Pickwick comes to Bath to take the waters, but his servant, Sam Weller, is not impressed, complaining that the water has 'a very strong flavour o' warm flat irons'. The Royal Crescent is also the setting for a chase between two characters, Dowler and Winkle.

Photograph 52994 (below) shows a busy but now vanished view of Bath. A few buildings on the left of the photograph survive, but the rest have gone, apart from the Abbey pinnacles in the distance. Second World War bombs and later demolition saw them off: the left side of Southgate Street was rebuilt in the 1960s, and the right side was replaced by the Mall shopping centre in 1971. The tower in the background was the Georgian St James's Church of 1768, whose blitzed ruins were finally demolished in 1957.

SOUTHGATE STREET 1904 52994

Photograph 57721, below, shows a line of Bath chairs waiting for customers outside the Pump Room. Bath chairs were invented by James Heath of Bath around 1750. They were used to bring sick and frail people to take the waters at the Pump Room or to

BATH CHAIRS OUTSIDE THE PUMP ROOM 1907 57721

use the baths, and became very popular; by the mid 19th century they had largely replaced the sedan chair which was the previous method of transport. The advantage of the Bath chair over the sedan chair was that only one person was needed to move it.

BATHEASTON, HIGH STREET c1960 B308019

The main road from London follows the old Roman road of the Fosse Way through Batheaston into Bath, shown in photograph B308019, above. Trams, originally horse-drawn, once ran along the same route. Down the street in the photograph stands Batheaston House, with its many chimneys; it was originally the home of the Walters family, 18th-century cloth merchants.

'Beau' Nash, the Master of Ceremonies of fashionable society in Bath, expected visitors to the city to follow a strict code of rules. Although the rule forbidding the wearing of swords in the city was very much of its time, he was also in line with 21st-century thinking when he forbade smoking in certain public places.

After the Roman legions left Britain in the early 5th century, the fortunes of Aquae Sulis declined and the Roman baths fell into ruins. In AD577 the 'Anglo-Saxon Chronicle' reports that the town, along with the old Roman towns in the areas of Gloucester and Cirencester, fell to the Saxon warlords Cuthwine and Ceawlin, after a mighty battle at nearby Dyrham; no less than three British kings were killed in this encounter.

The beautiful, tiny church of Charlcombe (photograph 57754, below) still seems far from the heart of the city that lies barely two miles away at the foot of the hill. It is dedicated to St Mary the Virgin and constructed of local limestone, and has a most unusual stone bell turret, battlemented and carried on big corbels. Victorian restorers rebuilt much of the church's ancient fabric and, more recently, fine oak pews from the Robert Thompson workshops in Yorkshire have been installed.

CHARLCOMBE, THE CHURCH 1907 57754

One of the most fascinating archaeological discoveries in Bath in recent years has been a large quantity of 'curse tablets' dating from the Roman period; they are usually described as being made of lead, but actually have a high tin content. These tablets are made up from thin, rectangular sheets upon which a text was inscribed with a pointed instrument. The tablet was then rolled or folded and deposited in the hot spring of the baths. They most commonly relate to thefts, as of clothing, or money, from the changing rooms at the baths, or a lost love, and are requests to the deity Sulis to punish the wrongdoer, usually by the denial of sleep, by causing normal bodily functions to cease, or even by death:

May he who has stolen Vilbia from me become as liquid as water …

Docilianus … to the most holy goddess Sulis. I curse him who has stolen my hooded cloak, whether man or woman, whether slave or free, that … the goddess Sulis inflict death upon … and not allow him sleep or children now and in the future, until he has brought my hooded cloak to the temple of her divinity.

To the goddess Sulis Minerva. I ask your most sacred majesty that you take vengeance on those who have done [me] wrong, that you permit them neither sleep…

The medieval town of Bath was a prosperous one, being in the centre of a wool and cloth producing area with a river to carry exports to Bristol. Unfortunately very little of the medieval town survives, apart from its street plan. The abbey is by far the most important medieval structure, but otherwise there is only the much-altered 15th-century Church of St Mary Magdalene and a small portion of the town wall. There is also very little left from the Tudor and Stuart periods.

THE PARAGON 1911 63684

GREAT PULTENEY STREET 1890 25130

Named after William Pulteney, Earl of Bath, and designed by Thomas Baldwin, Great Pulteney Street has been described as the finest street in Europe. It is pictured in winter in photograph 25130 (above): a dusting of snow covers the ground and carriage drivers await a summons to take residents into town. The horses are now gone and the fountain has changed, but otherwise the street looks much the same today.

The architect John Wood the Elder planned the North and South Parades as part of an area based on the architecture of ancient Rome. Terrace Walk, with the abbey behind, ran between the 18th-century Harrison's and Lindsay's Assembly Rooms, and the wide pavements were for promenading. The Assembly Rooms were badly damaged during the Second World War, but have been faithfully restored; the basement now houses one of the world's finest collections of costume.

In 1013 the Danish Sweyn Forkbeard (father of the future King Canute) accepted the fealty at Bath of the powerful Anglo-Saxon leaders of the west of England, who had lost patience with their king, Edward 'the Unready'. The chronicles record that 'King Sweyn went from there to Wallingford, over the Thames to Bath, and stayed there with his troops; Ealdorman Aethelmaer came, and the western thegns with him. They all bowed to Sweyn and gave hostages'.

The Kennet and Avon Canal, authorised by Act of Parliament in 1794 and opened in 1810, linked Bristol with London, cutting a canal from the Avon in Bath to the Kennet, which was then canalised to the Thames. Photograph 35759 (below) shows the view from the canal towpath, looking north to the Bathwick Hill bridge in Bathwick with the backs of Sydney Buildings on the right. The waterway quickly became a great success and in its heyday annually carried some 350,000 tons of freight. However, the railways heralded its decline, and it was taken over by the Great Western Railway.

ON THE CANAL 1895 35759

Designed by Robert Adam and built between 1769 and 1774, the Palladian-style Pulteney-Bridge was built for Sir William Pulteney to link his Bathwick estate to the city (see photograph B33155, below). Adam adapted Palladio's own design for a bridge

PULTENEY BRIDGE c1965 B33155

with shops and houses to produce an elegant masterpiece. However, the commission ruined the builder, and parts had to be reconstructed as early as 1804. This bridge is the only work of Robert Adam in Bath.

THE ROMAN BATHS 1897 40789

Just outside Bath at Claverton Down is Claverton Manor, now the American Museum. This was founded in 1961 to increase Anglo-American understanding. Eighteen rooms are set out with American furniture dating from the 17th to the 19th century, including the Shaker room with examples of classic Shaker design and furniture, offering visitors a chance to step back in time. The museum holds an important collection of American quilts, and also has exhibits of the arts and customs of Native Americans and the opening up of the American West, including a prairie wagon in the grounds.

Despite the rise to prominence of Bath as a spa in the 18th century, the waters had in fact been taken since the 15th century. The King's Bath was the focus of this activity, mostly of immersion but also of a certain amount of drinking the waters. The 1597 spring, or well top, of the bath was replicated a century ago as its centrepiece, and there is a famous print of men and women enjoying themselves in the King's Bath together - this would have been viewed as shocking behaviour by 'Beau' Nash, the Arbiter of Elegance.

The popularity of Bath increased dramatically in the mid 18th century after Dr William Oliver, an authority on gout, opened the Royal Mineral Water Hospital offering treatments for that complaint. Dr Oliver's other claim to fame is that he invented the Bath Oliver biscuit; he was an anti-obesity campaigner and these lightweight biscuits were an early slimming aid. It is said that Dr Oliver left the recipe to his coachman, Atkins, after his death, with the sum of £100 and a large quantity of flour. Atkins opened a shop in Green Street to sell the biscuits, and became a rich man. The business later passed to a Mr Norris, who sold out to a baker called Carter. After two further changes of ownership, the Bath Oliver biscuit recipe passed to James Fortt in the 1950s. In 1952 over 80,000 biscuits a day were being made in Bath, but although they are still available, they are no longer made in the city.

UNION STREET 1923 73964

The Roman bath complex and temple was ruined by flooding when water levels rose in the 4th century; as the level of the River Avon rose, the drains became blocked with mud and silt. At the end of the Roman period in Britain the baths were not repaired and fell into ruins. The site of the temple of Sul-Minerva became a dumping ground for rubbish, and in later

THE ROMAN BATHS 1901 46468

years was used as a Saxon graveyard. The 8th-century Anglo-Saxon poem 'The Ruin' is believed to be a description of the ruined grandeur of Roman Bath at that time: 'Wondrous is this masonry, shattered by the Fates. The fortifications have given way, the buildings raised by giants are crumbling. The city fell to earth.'

THE ROYAL CRESCENT c1965 B33174

The extraordinary Royal Crescent, designed by John Wood the Younger, was built between 1767 and 1774 and was probably the first crescent in England. It is a breathtaking monumental semi-ellipse of 30 houses, with 114 giant columns to the two upper floors in its prodigious length of 538ft (see photograph B33174, above).

Bath was attacked by the Luftwaffe during the Second World War as part of the campaign known as the 'Baedeker raids'; these were raids deliberately aimed at some of Britain's most historic cities, chosen from the Baedeker guide books, and were an attempt by the Germans to lower British morale. Between the evening of 25 April and the morning of 27 April, Bath was the subject of three air raids which damaged or destroyed more than 19,000 buildings and killed more than 400 people. Much damage was done to the Royal Crescent, the Circus, the Paragon and Assembly Rooms, and part of the south side of Queen Square was destroyed. All the damaged buildings have since been reconstructed.

The William Herschel Museum in New King Street celebrates the achievements of William Herschel and his sister Caroline who lived in this building, both of whom were not only talented musicians but also astronomical scientists. William Herschel (1738-1822) became the Director of Music in Bath and held regular concerts at the Pump Room and the Assembly Rooms, where he was well known for his musical compositions, but he was also a distinguished astronomer. Herschel extended the science of telescope building, and it was from this house in Bath, using a telescope of his own design, that Herschel discovered the planet Uranus in 1781. He was able to claim 'I have looked further into space than any other human being did before me', and his work helped to double the known size of the solar system. The patron of the museum, Patrick Moore, said: 'William Herschel was the first man to give a reasonably correct picture of the shape of our star-system or galaxy; he was the best telescope-maker of his time, and possibly the greatest observer who ever lived'. Herschel's sister Caroline also made a significant contribution to astrological knowledge - see page 43.

UNION STREET 1914 67454

The author Jane Austen lived in Bath from 1801 until 1806. Two of her novels, 'Northanger Park' and 'Persuasion' were set in the city, and give an interesting perspective on the social life of Bath in the early 19th century. However, although the city proved an inspiration for her pen, Jane Austen disliked Bath, and the 'elegant stupidity' of its dinner parties, and once wrote to her sister Cassandra: 'It will be two years tomorrow since we left Bath for Clifton, with what happy feelings of escape'. In 'Persuasion' she has Sir Walter Elliot saying 'There certainly were a dreadful multitude of ugly women in Bath; as for the men! they were infinitely worse'.

Bath is now known for the grace and elegance of its buildings, and became famous as a centre of fashion and taste, but was somewhat different at one time. Bath's famous architect John Wood described the scene before the city was transformed: 'Soil of all sorts, and even carrion, were cast and laid in the streets, and the pigs turned out by day to feed and rout among it; butchers killed and dressed their cattle at their own doors; people washed every kind of thing they had to make clean at the common conduits in the open streets ....'

The painter Thomas Gainsborough (1727-88) lived in Bath for 15 years during his 'peak period', when he painted 'Blue Boy' and other major works. When he arrived, in 1759, Gainsborough was already an artist of recognised ability, but by the time he left, he had become one of the most famous artists of his time. His career was made during his time in the city, where his ability to capture a likeness quickly made him popular with high-profile aristocratic clients with busy social lives and hectic schedules. Examples of his work are held in the Victoria Art Gallery.

Caroline Herschel, whose work is also commemorated in Bath's William Herschel Museum, assisted her brother William in the manufacture of his improved telescopes and shared his passion for astronomy; she also helped him to develop the more mathematical approach to the science which is the norm today. Although Caroline first worked as her brother's apprentice, as her knowledge and expertise grew she began to work increasingly on her own. In 1783, Caroline Herschel discovered three new nebulae (the hazy clouds where stars form). She was the first woman to discover a comet, and in fact between 1786 and 1797 she discovered a total of eight comets. In her later years, Caroline catalogued every discovery that she and William had made; two of the astronomical catalogues published by her are still in use today. She died in 1848 at the age of 98.

THE ABBEY AND THE PUMP ROOM 1929 82332

EDGAR BUILDINGS 1935 86804

During the Civil War, the battle of Lansdown was fought on the outskirts of Bath on 5 July 1643. The Royalists, under Lord Ralph Hopton, charged the Parliamentarian forces under the command of Sir William Waller, forcing them to retreat a short distance to a second defence line, but at such a high cost in casualties that the Royalist army had to retire to Devizes in Wiltshire; the casualties in the Parliamentarian forces, however, were much lighter. Sir Bevil Grenville, the leader of the Cornish infantry on the Royalist side, was killed at Lansdown, where the site of the battle is marked by a monument.

The entrance block of the Theatre Royal was formed from 'Beau' Nash's first house in Bath. He later moved to what is now the Popjoy's restaurant, which is named after Nash's mistress, Juliana Popjoy. Nash and Juliana separated, but she returned to nurse him in the last years of his life.

The Old Bridge across the Avon, shown in photograph 19590, below, was built in 1754 and incorporated an earlier bridge from the 14th century. It was demolished and replaced in 1966 by a modern road bridge. The crenellated arches in the background of the photograph are of the splendid medieval-style railway line of the 1840s, which follows the line of the old Roman walls and carries Brunel's railway above the flood plain of the Avon to the city station, just to the left.

THE OLD BRIDGE 1887 19590

SPORTING BATH

During rugby matches between Bath and Llanelli, a 3ft-tall rag doll is hung on one of the uprights to 'watch' the game. After the game, the doll wears the colours of the winning team until the next encounter.

Bath City's Twerton Park has been home to three teams in recent times. Bath City own and play at the ground but they were also landlords to football league side Bristol Rovers for a number of years in the 1980s and 1990s, and Team Bath, the university football team, currently play at the ground.

Bath Rugby Club has produced many international players over the years. Herbert Fuller is generally thought to have been the first, in an 1882 game against Scotland. The first non-English international from the club was Ian Lumsden, who was selected for Scotland in 1947.

Perhaps the most successful footballer to come from Bath was Tony Book, whose story is surely unique in English football. Book was born in Bath in 1934, and played over 400 games for his home-town club. In 1964 his former Bath City manager Malcolm Allison took him to football league side Plymouth Argyle, where he played 84 games, making his league debut at the age of 30! His career continued to flourish when he was again recruited by Allison to join him at first division Manchester City. He was installed as team captain, and on 11 May 1968 led the team to the league championship. More success followed as he led Manchester City to an FA Cup win in 1969, and they won the European Cup in 1970. He was rewarded with a share of the 'Football Writers' Player of the Year' award in 1969. Later as manager of Manchester City he led them to a League Cup success in 1976.

Horse racing has taken place in the Bath area since at least 1728. Racing took place at Claverton Down until 1796, and started at Lansdown in 1811. Bath racecourse is the highest course in Britain, being nearly 800ft above sea level. The course hosts the 'Bathwick Tyres' Ladies' Derby, Europe's richest race for amateur lady jockeys.

Amongst the former pupils of Monkton Combe School, just outside Bath, are two Olympic medal winners. William Laurie (1948) and Rowley Douglas (2000) both won gold medals for rowing.

QUIZ QUESTIONS

Answers on page 50.

1. Why is an olive tree carved on the west front of Bath Abbey?

2. How did Milsom Street get its name?

3. Which garden ornaments, formerly the property of Napoleon Bonaparte, can be found in Bath?

4. By what name is Bath Abbey sometimes known?

5. By what name are residents of Bath known?

6. What was granted to Bath in 1590?

7. What is a Bath Chap?

8. Which powerful Bath personage is supposed to have inspired a character in Henry Fielding's novel 'Tom Jones'?

9. Who made his name and fortune - legally - by 'picking pockets' with a paintbrush in 18th-century Bath?

10. What is the connection between Bath and a felt mountain?

RECIPE

BATH GROUND RICE PUDDING

Ingredients
225g/8oz shortcrust pastry
50g/2oz ground rice
25g/1oz sugar
275ml/½ pint single cream
275ml/½ pint milk
2 eggs
25g/1oz butter
1 teaspoon sherry, or a few drops of vanilla essence if preferred
Freshly ground nutmeg

Line a 20cm (8in) flan tin with the shortcrust pastry and bake blind at 190 degrees C/375 degrees F/Gas Mark 5 for 15 minutes.

Put the milk and cream into a saucepan, sprinkle in the ground rice and sugar, and cook in a double boiler (stand the pan inside a larger pan half filled with boiling water, over heat), whisking all the time to prevent lumps forming. Simmer for 5 minutes, and remove from the heat when thickened.

Cool the mixture, then beat in the eggs, butter and sherry or vanilla. Fill the pastry case and bake at 160 degrees C/325 degrees F/ Gas Mark 3 for about 30 minutes. Grate some fresh nutmeg over the top before serving.

RECIPE

BATH BUNS

Bath Buns are thought to have been invented by Dr Oliver, who also devised the plain Bath Oliver biscuit. They were originally topped with 'confits', caraway seeds that had been dipped into boiling sugar, but this flavour is not to modern tastes and a crushed sugar topping is used instead. Bath buns were a great favourite of Jane Austen when she lived in the city.

Ingredients
15g/½ oz fresh yeast, or 10g/ ¼ oz dried yeast
1 teaspoon salt
300ml/½ pint tepid milk
350g/12oz plain flour
100g/4oz butter
75g/3oz caster sugar
2 eggs, beaten
50g/2oz candied peel, chopped
50g/2oz crushed lump sugar

Cream the yeast with one teaspoonful of the sugar and add to the tepid milk. (If using dried yeast, mix with the sugar and half the milk. Leave in a warm place until frothy, then add the rest of the milk.) Put the flour in a bowl and pour the yeast mixture into a well in the middle. Leave until frothy.

Cream the butter and the rest of the sugar, add the egg, reserving a little to glaze, and work into the dough. Reserve a little peel for decoration, then add the rest to the dough. Cover the dough with a cloth and leave in a warm place to rise for about 40 minutes.

Turn out and knead, then shape into buns about 5-7.5 (2-3 inches) across and place on a greased baking sheet, well spaced out. Leave to rise for a further 15-20 minutes, then brush with the rest of the egg, sprinkle with the coarsely crushed sugar and a little chopped peel. Bake in a preheated oven for about 30 minutes, at 180 degrees C/350 degrees F/Gas Mark 4.

QUIZ ANSWERS

1. An olive tree and crown surmounted by a mitre, carved in stone, can be seen on the west front of Bath Abbey. This commemorates Bishop Oliver King, who restored the abbey in the late 15th century.

2. Milsom Street was named after Daniel Milsom, a wine cooper who owned the land on which the street was built.

3. On each side of the bandstand in Victoria Park (see photograph 73971, page 52) are stone canopies protecting marble vases. The inscription tells us they were the gift of the Emperor Napoleon Bonaparte in 1805 to his Empress, Josephine. They were brought to England as spoils of war, and were given to the park in 1874.

4. 'The Lantern of England' - its 52 windows make the interior exceptionally light.

5. Bathonians.

6. Bath was granted city status in 1590.

7. A Bath Chap is the name given to a local delicacy, the salted and smoked lower half of a pig's cheeks. It is still sold from a stall in Bath's Guildhall covered market.

8. Ralph Allen, who lived at Prior Park. The author Henry Fielding was a frequent guest there, and is believed to have used Ralph Allen as the model for Squire Allworthy in 'Tom Jones'.

9. The artist Thomas Gainsborough, who made his fortune and his name by painting portraits of the wealthy and fashionable during Bath's social season, a business he referred to as 'picking pockets in the portrait way'. To maximize profits, Gainsborough had his sister, Mary Gibson, move her millinery business to the same building as his studio. He would send his sitters to her shop to accessorise themselves with her wares before being painted.

10. The pop duo Goldfrapp, whose members, Alison Goldfrap and Will Gregory, are from Bath. 'Felt Mountain' was the name of their first album, which was released in the winter of 2000 to much acclaim, and was nominated for the Mercury Music Prize in 2001.

THE FERNLEY HOTEL 1935 86800A

VICTORIA PARK 1920 73971

FRANCIS FRITH

PIONEER VICTORIAN PHOTOGRAPHER

Francis Frith, founder of the world-famous photographic archive, was a complex and multi-talented man. A devout Quaker and a highly successful Victorian businessman, he was philosophical by nature and pioneering in outlook. By 1855 he had already established a wholesale grocery business in Liverpool, and sold it for the astonishing sum of £200,000, which is the equivalent today of over £15,000,000. Now in his thirties, and captivated by the new science of photography, Frith set out on a series of pioneering journeys up the Nile and to the Near East.

INTRIGUE AND EXPLORATION

He was the first photographer to venture beyond the sixth cataract of the Nile. Africa was still the mysterious 'Dark Continent', and Stanley and Livingstone's historic meeting was a decade into the future. The conditions for picture taking confound belief. He laboured for hours in his wicker dark-room in the sweltering heat of the desert, while the volatile chemicals fizzed dangerously in their trays. Back in London he exhibited his photographs and was 'rapturously cheered' by members of the Royal Society. His reputation as a photographer was made overnight.

VENTURE OF A LIFE-TIME

By the 1870s the railways had threaded their way across the country, and Bank Holidays and half-day Saturdays had been made obligatory by Act of Parliament. All of a sudden the working man and his family were able to enjoy days out, take holidays, and see a little more of the world.

With typical business acumen, Francis Frith foresaw that these new tourists would enjoy having souvenirs to commemorate their days out. For the next thirty years he travelled the country by train and by pony and trap, producing fine photographs of seaside resorts and beauty spots that were keenly bought by millions of Victorians. These prints were painstakingly pasted into family albums and pored over during the dark nights of winter, rekindling precious memories of summer excursions. Frith's studio was soon supplying retail shops all over the country, and by 1890 F Frith & Co had become the greatest specialist photographic publishing company in the world, with over 2,000 sales outlets, and pioneered the picture postcard.

FRANCIS FRITH'S LEGACY

Francis Frith had died in 1898 at his villa in Cannes, his great project still growing. By 1970 the archive he created contained over a third of a million pictures showing 7,000 British towns and villages.

Frith's legacy to us today is of immense significance and value, for the magnificent archive of evocative photographs he created provides a unique record of change in the cities, towns and villages throughout Britain over a century and more. Frith and his fellow studio photographers revisited locations many times down the years to update their views, compiling for us an enthralling and colourful pageant of British life and character.

We are fortunate that Frith was dedicated to recording the minutiae of everyday life. For it is this sheer wealth of visual data, the painstaking chronicle of changes in dress, transport, street layouts, buildings, housing and landscape that captivates us so much today, offering us a powerful link with the past and with the lives of our ancestors.

Computers have now made it possible for Frith's many thousands of images to be accessed almost instantly. The archive offers every one of us an opportunity to examine the places where we and our families have lived and worked down the years. Its images, depicting our shared past, are now bringing pleasure and enlightenment to millions around the world a century and more after his death.

For further information visit: www.francisfrith.com

INTERIOR DECORATION

Frith's photographs can be seen framed and as giant wall murals in thousands of pubs, restaurants, hotels, banks, retail stores and other public buildings throughout Britain. These provide interesting and attractive décor, generating strong local interest and acting as a powerful reminder of gentler days in our increasingly busy and frenetic world.

FRITH PRODUCTS

All Frith photographs are available as prints and posters in a variety of different sizes and styles. In the UK we also offer a range of other gift and stationery products illustrated with Frith photographs, although many of these are not available for delivery outside the UK – see our web site for more information on the products available for delivery in your country.

THE INTERNET

Over 100,000 photographs of Britain can be viewed and purchased on the Frith web site. The web site also includes memories and reminiscences contributed by our customers, who have personal knowledge of localities and of the people and properties depicted in Frith photographs. If you wish to learn more about a specific town or village you may find these reminiscences fascinating to browse. Why not add your own comments if you think they would be of interest to others? See **www.francisfrith.com**

PLEASE HELP US BRING FRITH'S PHOTOGRAPHS TO LIFE

Our authors do their best to recount the history of the places they write about. They give insights into how particular towns and villages developed, they describe the architecture of streets and buildings, and they discuss the lives of famous people who lived there. But however knowledgeable our authors are, the story they tell is necessarily incomplete.

Frith's photographs are so much more than plain historical documents. They are living proofs of the flow of human life down the generations. They show real people at real moments in history; and each of those people is the son or daughter of someone, the brother or sister, aunt or uncle, grandfather or grandmother of someone else. All of them lived, worked and played in the streets depicted in Frith's photographs.

We would be grateful if you would give us your insights into the places shown in our photographs: the streets and buildings, the shops, businesses and industries. Post your memories of life in those streets on the Frith website: what it was like growing up there, who ran the local shop and what shopping was like years ago; if your workplace is shown tell us about your working day and what the building is used for now. Read other visitors' memories and reconnect with your shared local history and heritage. With your help more and more Frith photographs can be brought to life, and vital memories preserved for posterity, and for the benefit of historians in the future.

Wherever possible, we will try to include some of your comments in future editions of our books. Moreover, if you spot errors in dates, titles or other facts, please let us know, because our archive records are not always completely accurate—they rely on 140 years of human endeavour and hand-compiled records. You can email us using the contact form on the website.

Thank you!

For further information, trade, or author enquiries please contact us at the address below:

The Francis Frith Collection, Frith's Barn, Teffont, Salisbury, Wiltshire, England SP3 5QP.

Tel: +44 (0)1722 716 376 Fax: +44 (0)1722 716 881

e-mail: sales@francisfrith.co.uk **www.francisfrith.com**